JAAZ Nspiration

Rejuvenation of Mind, Body, and Soul for Teens

My 30-Day Journey of Spiritual Self-Discovery

Jacqueline Marie Norris, M.A.Ed

JAAZ Nspiration

Rejuvenation of Mind, Body, and Soul for Teens

My 30-Day Journey of Spiritual Self-Discovery

Jacqueline Marie Norris, M.A.Ed

Published by:
Jaaz Creative Designs

Copyright © 2020 by Jacqueline Marie Norris
San Francisco, California

Jacqueline Marie Norris, M.A.Ed, asserts the moral right to be identified as the author of this book.

All rights reserved. No part of this publication may be reproduced, distributed, or transmitted in any form or by any means, including photocopying, recording, or other electronic or mechanical methods, without the prior written permission of the publisher, except in the case of brief quotations embodied in critical reviews and certain other noncommercial uses permitted by copyright law. For permission requests, write to the publisher, addressed "Attention: Permissions Coordinator," at the address below.

Jaaz Creative Designs
PO BOX 347217
San Francisco, CA 94134
jaazworld@gmail.com

Cover Design: Jacqueline Marie Norris
Cover Illustration: Zeeshan Shahid
Internal Illustration: Kisa Uyadermont
Content Editor: Rikki Norris
Editor: Leesha Langlois

Book Concept and Cover Art Inspired by:
Curtis Leon Jones, III

Jaaz Nspiration Supporters:
Fatt Sak Records
JAAZWORLD.COM
JN Outreach Foundation, Inc.
Evergreen Baptist Church, San Francisco, CA
Without Walls International Ministries

Written and Printed within the United States of America

ISBN-13: 978-0-9998703-2-7

PREFACE

As a teen you may be feeling or may be having mixed emotions. Feelings of growing up yet not being recognized as you transition and grow in age. Today, I encourage you to stand up, claim your heritage as a child of God, be a person of strong courage, demonstrate traits of faith, and be the one to make a difference in the world, your environment, your community, and in your home!

While on this 30-Day journey, make it a point to focus yourself and your energy on your transition and growth. If there are any negative behaviors, feelings of insecurity, anxiousness, or anything that is controlling your thoughts I urge you to release those emotions as you embark on this journey.

This journey is personal and no one but you will know if you have inserted the appropriate amount of effort, applied enough energy, or if you grew from past experiences. As you read each daily entry allow your mind to be silent so that you can be open and willing to recognize God, His voice, His love, and His mercy. As you move towards the end of the next 30 days make it a point to take time to thank God for creating you, pray constantly for change, and commit to being a good role model for those who yearn to be like you or shall I say like the God in you. Last but not least, always remember that no matter what is going on in your world or your life God is in control (Reference Job 12:10; Proverbs 16:9; Psalm 115:3) and that He is there to protect and guide you (Reference Joshua 1:9; Matthew 6:24; Psalm 34:4) as you welcome each day.

INTRODUCTION

In our society, many people struggle with time; be it finding time, making time, having time, or how to use time. Many people your age find themselves busy with school, family, social activity or employment. This 30-day journey will allow you to make time for time. If you make the commitment to read a page each day and do the exercises, day by day you will find that you do have time for time and you will begin to look forward to the time you set aside to reflect. You will be able to connect or reconnect with God, you can spend time in prayer or learn to pray, you will be able to read the parts of Bible that apply to you, and lastly you can use this time to encourage yourself and monitor your own personal or spiritual growth.

Self-acknowledgment, Self-awareness, and Self-appreciation are three qualities that are vital to spiritual and human growth. These are three areas that will help you as you learn to set goals and aim for achievement not just while on this 30-Day Journey but in life as well.

While on this Journey if you dedicate the time, you will see a change in you, your attitude, and more importantly you will discover things about you that you did not know.

Generally speaking, every action causes us to react or shift our behavior in one direction or another. As you start this journey, I recommend that you intentionally set out to grow closer with God, get in touch with your emotions, and release any level of internal stress, anxiety, or fear you may have.

Let this journey open your mind to a new perspective and shift your behavior, your thought process, and your future actions.

Enjoy the journey as you rejuvenate your mind, body, and soul.

PRAYER

May God bless you as you embark on your journey of self-discovery. May He give you patience and strength along with self-determination as you explore what it takes to be a teen/youth striving to make progressive changes in your own life and contribute to the life of those in your inner circle.

In Jesus' name I pray this prayer. Amen!

Now before you begin, take a moment right now to say, "thank you Lord". Thank him for your past experiences, thank him for the lessons that you have learned, thank him for who you will be after you complete the 30-Day Journey, thank him for the people he sent to you, thank him for the people he removed from your life, thank him for where he is taking you, and thank him for the opportunity to take this journey as you discover your truth.

In the space below write about or list anything that you are interested in learning or changing about yourself while on this journey of self-discovery.

The Journey Begins

Jaaz Nspiration

Day One:
Enjoy Life and Its Moments

There is value in living and taking time to enjoy and be in the moment.

Today go out of your way to hug someone, say good morning, lend a hand, check-in with someone, say hello, make eye contact, shake a hand etc. All of those actions are relevant in making memories and enhancing someone's life, including yours.

Wisdom Key: Spending 5 additional minutes doing one or all of these activities will open your mind to freedom and allow you to extend joy to others.

Use your phone, Bible app, or physical Bible to read the following scriptures:

Luke 6:35; Romans 12:10; Galatians 5:13

Do these scriptures call you to do something or change a current behavior? ☐ Yes ☐ No
If yes, explain:

My Journey!

In the evening, write a statement that describes what you did to enjoy or live in the moment, include how it made you feel. If you are not normally a person who enjoys personal contact this activity may cause you to feel uncomfortable, and that is ok.

_____
_____
_____
_____
_____
_____
_____
_____
_____

Prayer: Lord, thank you for giving me this opportunity to extend love and to share kindness. Thank you for guiding me and letting me see your blessings in every situation. Amen.

What did you learn about yourself today?

You Are Worthy & GOD Lives In You

You Are Loved & You Are Chosen

Write or draw your expression/emotions above.

Day Two: Taking a Stand

When you are not clear in your thought, speech, or action as it relates to a moral or ethical standards/behavior you may find yourself compromising the rights and freedoms of yourself and others.

When that happens hostility, anger, and malice may appear. Making decisions based on human values and respect is always a good choice! Being aware and understanding your values are critical when it comes to taking a stand.

Action: How do your values impact your decision making process and Why?

Use your phone, Bible app, or physical Bible to read the following scriptures:

Matthew 7:12; Philippians 2:3; Proverbs 16:9; James 1:6-8

Do these scriptures call you to do something or change a current behavior? ☐ Yes ☐ No If yes, explain:

My Journey.

Write a statement in two or more sentences that describes a time when you made a good choice related to human value or respect. Also include how you felt or your perception of how the other person(s) felt as it relates to your action(s).

_____
_____
_____
_____
_____
_____
_____
_____

Prayer: Lord, thank you for showing me how important respect is. Please guide me to be clear in my actions so that I do not disrespect the values or rights of others. Amen.

What did you learn about yourself today?

You Are Worthy & GOD Lives In You

You Are Loved & You Are Chosen

Write or draw your expression/emotions above.

Day Three: Grace and Mercy

My Journey.

God's grace and mercy gives us the ability to do the impossible. That same grace and mercy heals broken hearts, mends relationships, restores love, offers forgiveness, and increases our faith.

Action: Today extend and accept grace and mercy in the form of forgiveness to/from someone who needs it so that you can be free to Love and Live!

Use your phone, Bible app, or physical Bible to read the following scriptures:

Numbers 14:18; Luke 6:37; Luke 17:4; 1 John 1:9

Do these scriptures call you to do something or change a current behavior? ☐ Yes ☐ No If yes, explain:

Write a statement that describes a time when you needed forgiveness from God, a person(s), or yourself.

Knowing that God has extended forgiveness to you even when you did not deserve it; if there is a person(s) who desires your forgiveness in two or more sentences describe how will you handle the situation(s)?

_____
_____
_____
_____
_____
_____
_____
_____
_____
_____

Prayer: Thank you for always forgiving me when I need it. Help me to remember to forgive others too. Amen.

What did you learn about yourself today?

You Are Worthy & GOD Lives In You

You Are Loved & You Are Chosen

Write or draw your expression/emotions above.

Day Four: Love Repairs Relationships

With true FAMILY (By blood or by choice), love has the power to supersede manifested issues, misunderstandings, hurt feelings, abuse, and verbal backlash. Consider renewing or creating closer relationships when the opportunity presents itself.

When you openly extend love to your family and friends you will be able to freely forgive, release, and LIVE in a state of happiness!

Wisdom Key: Love can open the door of internal and spiritual freedom.

Use your phone, Bible app, or physical Bible to read the following scriptures:

James 1:19; Ephesians 4:32; Romans 12:12; Ephesians 4:2

Do these scriptures call you to do something or change a current behavior? ☐ Yes ☐ No If yes, explain:

My Journey.

Write a statement that describes a time when a family relationship was broken or strained. In your statement include your actions/participation or note if you were a witness.

State your feelings and describe if it made you angry or sorrowful.

_____
_____
_____
_____
_____
_____
_____
_____
_____

Prayer: Lord, help me to not be the person to break trust or bring harm to a family member. Lord allow me to be in healthy relationships with my family and friends. Amen.

What did you learn about yourself today?

You Are Worthy & GOD Lives In You

You Are Loved & You Are Chosen

Write or draw your expression/emotions above.

Day Five: Express Gratitude

My Journey.

As this week comes to an end, use this time to be thankful for what you have, where you are, for your family/ friends, and for the protection as well as the forgiveness that God has granted you. With the potential of tragedy all around you, it is safe to say you are definitely blessed to see another day!

Wisdom Key:
GRATEFUL is an adjective which means **THANKFUL**. **GRATITUDE** is a noun which means **THANKS**.

Use your phone, Bible app, or physical Bible to read the following scriptures:

1 Corinthians 1:4-5; Matthew 6:14-15; 1 Thessalonians 5:16-18; Ephesians 1:71; Chronicles 16:34-35

Do these scriptures call you to do something or change a current behavior? ☐ Yes ☐ No If yes, explain:

Write a statement that describes a memorable event or situation where you were in danger or felt fearful but the end result left you feeling thankful or fully knowing that you received a blessing by a person or by God.

Think of a time when someone expressed gratitude to you. What was your reaction and why?

_____
_____
_____
_____
_____
_____
_____
_____
_____
_____

Prayer: Allow me to always see you and to be thankful. Please be a constant reminder of forgiveness to me as I seek peace in all situations. Amen.

What did you learn about yourself today?

You Are Worthy & GODLives In You

You Are Loved & You Are Chosen

Write or draw your expression/emotions above.

Day Six:
You Can Make It

May your day be filled with many blessings, love, accomplishment, and respect. As you progress through this day, please know that you have what it takes to overcome and rise above nonsense, defeat, guilt, pressures of life, and depression. Your cup is half full not half empty!

Wisdom Key: Your life matters and so do your feelings. Having a person to talk to can help you see things differently. It is ok to openly talk about things that make you sad or depressed.

Use your phone, Bible app, or physical Bible to read the following scriptures:

1 Peter 5:7; Matthew 6:25-27; James 1:2-4; Philippians 4:19

Do these scriptures call you to do something or change a current behavior? ☐ Yes ☐ No If yes, explain:

My Journey.

Think of a time when you achieved a goal you set or a goal that was set for you. Describe how that moment of achievement felt and what you did to celebrate that success.

_____
_____
_____
_____
_____
_____
_____
_____
_____

Prayer: Jesus, any time that I become sad or have feelings of depression please regulate my mind and shift my perspective so that I can focus on the good within me. Show me how to trust you and to love myself the way that you love me. Amen.

What did you learn about yourself today?

You Are Worthy & GOD Lives In You

You Are Loved & You Are Chosen

Write or draw your expression/emotions above.

Day Seven: Live a Life of Substance

Stay focused and away from negative thinking, attitudes, and behavior so that you can thrive and live a life of substance.

Success is not found in a man's (human) wallet, bank account, status, or possessions but in his/her heart and his/her actions. Each day walk in acceptance of newness!

Action: If you were able to trade (sacrifice) 3 of your personal items of great value in exchange for true love, wisdom, and happiness for you and your family what would those items be?

Use your phone, Bible app, or physical Bible to read the following scriptures:

Revelation 21:4; Philippians 2:5; Isaiah 54:4; John 15:10-12

Do these scriptures call you to do something or change a current behavior? ☐ Yes ☐ No If yes, explain:

My Journey.

Think of two people who provoke you to engage in negative thinking or behavior. In two sentences write what you can do to change that relationship so that it results in empowerment and not negativity. You can also include how you feel about the interaction(s).

_____
_____
_____
_____
_____
_____
_____
_____

Prayer: Lord thank you for my life. I appreciate what you have done for me, my family, and friends. Please help me to see that the real value in life includes my relationship with you Jesus. Amen.

What did you learn about yourself today?

Left border (vertical): You Are Worthy & GOD Lives In You

Right border (vertical): You Are Loved & You Are Chosen

Write or draw your expression/emotions above.

Day Eight: Remain Thankful

Life nor happiness is promised; therefore, be thankful for where you are at this very moment.

While you may not be where you want or expect to be someone is in a far worse situation than you. Never forget to pray for yourself, your family, friends, and the world daily!

Action: Write three phrases that state where you plan to be or how you want to feel about life within the next six months.

Use your phone, Bible app, or physical Bible to read the following scriptures:

Jeremiah 29:11-14; Zephaniah 3:17; Proverbs 16:3

Do these scriptures call you to do something or change a current behavior? ☐ Yes ☐ No If yes, explain:

My Journey.

Thinking back, where were you or how were you feeling about life 3 months or 1 year ago? Write a statement using 3 short sentences that describes those feelings or that moment.

_____
_____
_____
_____
_____
_____
_____
_____
_____
_____

Prayer: Thank you for waking me up and for giving me another chance to be better, do more, and learn. Please continue to watch over me and my family especially when things get rough. Amen.

What did you learn about yourself today?

You Are Worthy & GOD Lives In You

You Are Loved & You Are Chosen

Write or draw your expression/emotions above.

Day Nine: Give Yourself to Others

There comes a point in time when we all need someone. A helping hand, a kind word, a hug, a smile, or a compliment has the power to turn a bad day into a day of hope! Take time today to give someone hope; exchange love, offer your time, lend your attention, and strengthen a friendship.

Action: Write the name of 3 songs that you listen to that remind you of the need to have people who understand you in your corner or in your life.

Use your phone, Bible app, or physical Bible to read the following scriptures:

1 John 3:16; Hebrews 13:1-25 1 Corinthians 13:6-7; John 13:34-35

Do these scriptures call you to do something or change a current behavior? ☐ Yes ☐ No If yes, explain:

My Journey.

Think of your friend circle. Has there even been a time when a friend called or contacted you to talk about personal issues (such as relationships, home life, school, or personal feeling etc.)? Write at least two sentences that tell how you were able to help them.

_____
_____
_____
_____
_____
_____
_____
_____
_____
_____

Prayer: Lord, today as I reflect on my life I can see where you chose to love me. Please give me the ability to love others in that same way, freely, and without hesitation. Amen.

What did you learn about yourself today?

You Are Worthy & GOD Lives In You

You Are Loved & You Are Chosen

Write or draw your expression/emotions above.

Day Ten: Teach Love and Respect

Hatred, discrimination, and judgment are behaviors that are taught. These learned behaviors can destroy unity and relationships. Adults should teach their children and encourage their peers, inner circle, and those who they have influence over to be more loving, to display respect, and to be open minded! God wants us to embrace the differences in others.

Action: Document a time when you disrespected someone by calling them out of their name, made fun of their culture, or laughed at their difference or weakness.

Use your phone, Bible app, or physical Bible to read the following scriptures:

John 15:9-10; Romans 5:8; Jeremiah 31:3

Do these scriptures call you to do something or change a current behavior? ☐ Yes ☐ No If yes, explain:

My Journey.

Based on your Action response, other than apologizing what can you do or how would you change the narrative to flip the situation into a positive experience for you and that person/people?

_____
_____
_____
_____
_____
_____
_____
_____
_____
_____

Prayer: Lord, you created us all different. Help the people of the world to recognize our individual beauty and see the value of our colorless spirit. Thank you Lord for doing what no one else does, for loving without condition and judgement. Amen.

What did you learn about yourself today?

Left border (vertical): You Are Worthy & GOD Lives In You

Right border (vertical): You Are Loved & You Are Chosen

Write or draw your expression/emotions above.

Day Eleven: Uplift Others

As you start your day reflect on your previous blessings, achievements, successful events, and exciting memories. If you are feeling down use those thoughts to uplift your spirits. If you are already in good spirits share your joy with someone so that they can be uplifted and encouraged by your words and actions.

Action: Pick three encouraging words and use them today to change the mood, attitude, or feelings of three people. Document your achievement.

Use your phone, Bible app, or physical Bible to read the following scriptures:

Job 11:17-19; Romans 15:13; Ecclesiastes 3:12-13; Proverbs 16:3

Do these scriptures call you to do something or change a current behavior? ☐ Yes ☐ No If yes, explain:

My Journey.

Write a statement using two or three sentences that describes a time when you woke up feeling good and or excited. What can you do to recapture that feeling daily?

_____
_____
_____
_____
_____
_____
_____
_____
_____
_____
_____
_____

Prayer: Lord allow me to be the light for someone. Allow me to see that you are my light, my blessing, and my hope. Thank you for my achievements and for my many joyous moments. Amen.

What did you learn about yourself today?

You Are Worthy & GOD Lives In You

You Are Loved & You Are Chosen

Write or draw your expression/emotions above.

Day Twelve: Improve Health

Relaxing and releasing stress has the ability to improve your health, shift your perspective, and increase positive thinking.

When you feel tense take a few moments to inhale fresh air, quiet your mind, and release anything that feels draining or overwhelming.

In those anxious moments stand up, stretch your arms to the ceiling, and count to 10 while inhaling and exhaling at each count.

Action: Do you ever feel stress? If so, how do you deal with it?

Use your phone, Bible app, or physical Bible to read the following scriptures:

1 Peter 5:7; Philippians 4:6-7; 2 Timothy 1:7; Psalm 94:19

Do these scriptures call you to do something or change a current behavior? ☐ Yes ☐ No If yes, explain:

My Journey.

List three things that cause you stress, it can be a person, school, home life, family issues, social pressure etc.

Looking at those 3 names, things, or situations, is there anything that they all have in common? If so, what?

_____
_____
_____
_____
_____
_____
_____
_____
_____
_____
_____
_____

Prayer: Lord, help me to relax and not be angry. Please remove the stress triggers in my life so that I will not be distracted from my focus, my joy or my purpose. Amen.

What did you learn about yourself today?

You Are Worthy & GOD Lives In You

You Are Loved & You Are Chosen

Write or draw your expression/emotions above.

Day Thirteen: Trust Your Foundation

When faced with opposition, oppression, depression, or negativity we must remember that we are being tested. We must remember who we are, where we are going, where we came from, and most of all to whom we belong. Trouble, trials, and difficulty will not last forever. Stand on your foundation and wait for the Lord to heal, deliver, and to provide direction. He can help release feelings of bondage.

Action: Are you a victim of your own demise? Do you often think negative and then wonder why things do not end up better than they do?

Use your phone, Bible app, or physical Bible to read the following scriptures:

Proverbs 1:7; 1 Corinthians 1:25; James 1:5; Leviticus 19:3

Do these scriptures call you to do something or change a current behavior? ☐ Yes ☐ No If yes, explain:

My Journey.

Write an important statement or phrase that was said to you by someone in your life; something that will stick with you forever.

What piece of life advice would you give to someone younger than you to positively impact their future?

_____
_____
_____
_____
_____
_____
_____
_____
_____
_____
_____

Prayer: Lord, help me to rely on my foundation instead of looking at what I see on a daily basis. Show me how to trust in you. Amen.

What did you learn about yourself today?

You Are Worthy & GOD Lives In You

You Are Loved & You Are Chosen

Write or draw your expression/emotions above.

Day Fourteen: Reach Out to Others

It is always a good feeling when you uplift someone's spirit, be kind, or share an encouraging word. Sacrificing 5 to 10 minutes of your time reaching out to others can result in a life changing experience for you and the person you speak to!

Action: In two sentences jot down how the call (Listed under My Journey) made you feel. If the person you called shared any feelings with you about the call, you can write about that.

Use your phone, Bible app, or physical Bible to read the following scriptures:

Proverbs 19:17; Zechariah 7:9; Matthew 25:37-40; Psalm 41:1

Do these scriptures call you to do something or change a current behavior? ☐ Yes ☐ No If yes, explain:

My Journey.

Using your cell phone or your home phone call one person whom you have not spoken to within the last 14 days. Find out how they are doing and see if they are doing anything special for the weekend. By reaching out this evening, you can bring a smile to someone's face/heart and it may result in a blessing for you as well.

_____
_____
_____
_____
_____
_____
_____
_____
_____
_____

Prayer: Dear God, please keep me humble and remind me to always think of someone who has less or is going through a tough time. Amen.

What did you learn about yourself today?

You Are Worthy & GOD Lives In You

You Are Loved & You Are Chosen

Write or draw your expression/emotions above.

Day Fifteen: Press On

On the days when you feel like giving up due to lack of money, disappointment by friends, feeling unworthy of love, school has you frustrated, or family has you upset know that God is there waiting on you to call on Him. Ask God to help you withstand the trial, believe that he has the power, and watch your situation change for the better.

Wisdom Key: Life can present troubles and feelings of fear or anxiety. When your trust is placed in Jesus you can press on and make it through.

Use your phone, Bible app, or physical Bible to read the following scriptures:

Psalm 118:1; Daniel 2:23; Psalm7:17; Colossians 4:2

Do these scriptures call you to do something or change a current behavior? ☐ Yes ☐ No If yes, explain:

My Journey.

Take a few minutes, look in the mirror and in your outside voice say these words 3 times each in order, "I am worthy of love!", "I am worthy of life!", and "I am worthy of God's mercy!"

Write one sentence about how hearing you say those words made you feel.

_____
_____
_____
_____
_____
_____
_____
_____
_____

Prayer: Heavenly Father, thank you for forgiving me of my sins. Thank you for giving me another chance to experience your love in my life. Amen.

What did you learn about yourself today?

Left border (top to bottom): You Are Worthy & GOD Lives In You

Right border (top to bottom): You Are Loved & You Are Chosen

Write or draw your expression/emotions above.

Day Sixteen: Empowerment

My Journey.

It is really hard for most youths to be honest with themselves as well as each other. Someone may be contemplating or wrestling with thoughts of suicide or depression. Be aware, open your heart and mind, reach out to someone that you know may be having a hard time at home, with a parent, at school, struggling with gender decisions or dealing with a lack of food or housing. Try to redirect their path and be the encouragement that they may need to fight depression or suicidal thoughts.

Use your phone, Bible app, or physical Bible to read the following scriptures:

Jeremiah 29:11-13; Mark 10:27; Philippians 4:7; Psalm 46:1-3

Do these scriptures call you to do something or change a current behavior? ☐ Yes ☐ No If yes, explain:

Being a friend to someone does not mean that you have to agree with them. It is an opportunity to listen objectively and express compassion NOT pity.

A real friend tells the truth. Have you ever had a real friend tell you the truth even when you did not want to hear it? How did it make you feel? And why?

_____
_____
_____
_____
_____
_____
_____
_____
_____
_____

Prayer: Please Lord, help me to see who my real friends are. Amen.

What did you learn about yourself today?

You Are Worthy & GOD Lives In You

You Are Loved & You Are Chosen

Write or draw your expression/emotions above.

Day Seventeen: Release

Today is a new day. Release things that you have no control over and embrace the precious gifts of this day! Easy to say – Hard to do!

We like to believe that we are in control of our life. From time to time we are reminded that we are the character and not the director of our lives. Letting God handle your troubles is the best way to have joy and peace.

Action: If you could release or let go of one trouble right now, what would it be?

___

Use your phone, Bible app, or physical Bible to read the following scriptures:

1 Peter 5:7; Exodus 14:14; Psalm 94:19; Joshua 1-9; Psalm 23:4

Do these scriptures call you to do something or change a current behavior? ☐ Yes ☐ No If yes, explain:

My Journey.

If you were told that you were free to do anything you want in the world in the next 20 minutes without restriction for 20 hours, what would you do? And why?

_____
_____
_____
_____
_____
_____
_____
_____
_____
_____
_____
_____
_____

Prayer: I appreciate the idea of being free but I am learning that without you in my life I will never be 100% free. Please Lord help me realize that my freedom begins with you because of you. Amen.

What did you learn about yourself today?

Left border (vertical): You Are Worthy & GOD Lives In You

Right border (vertical): You Are Loved & You Are Chosen

Write or draw your expression/emotions above.

Day Eighteen: Remain Positive

When storms (challenges, difficulty, hurt feelings, or uncomfortable feelings) rage in your life, don't fret; the Rescuer is making a way for you.

Through struggle a lesson is being taught, lives are being changed, and growth is in process. Remain positive and know that troubles will come and go.

Action: Focus on two places that you go or have gone that make you feel happy and relaxed. Go there in your mind for 20 minutes.

Use your phone, Bible app, or physical Bible to read the following scriptures:

Philippians 4:8; Romans 12:2, Proverbs 2:25; Proverbs 17:22

Do these scriptures call you to do something or change a current behavior? ☐ Yes ☐ No If yes, explain:

My Journey.

Write two sentences that describe how you felt after taking 20 minutes to go to a zone where you did not feel anxious or rushed.

_____
_____
_____
_____
_____
_____
_____
_____
_____
_____
_____
_____

Prayer: God, I am thankful to have been places and done things that I can reflect on when things get tough. Please Lord, help me to make you the center of my joy and be the restart button that I need. Amen.

What did you learn about yourself today?

Left border (vertical): You Are Worthy & GOD Lives In You

Right border (vertical): You Are Loved & You Are Chosen

Write or draw your expression/emotions above.

Day Nineteen:
Make Time to Express and Display Love

May the love that runs through you be acknowledged, displayed, and expressed towards others on a daily basis not just on special occasions or when you feel like it.

Action: When you think of yourself, do you think of yourself as a person who deserves love? Do you think that love draws to you or runs away from you? Write your thoughts and keep in mind that Jesus died on the cross based on His love for you even before you were born.

Use your phone, Bible app, or physical Bible to read the following scriptures:

Romans 13:8; 1 John 2:9-10; Psalm 143:8; 1 John 4:8

Do these scriptures call you to do something or change a current behavior? ☐ Yes ☐ No If yes, explain:

My Journey.

Saying the words, I love you can be life changing. Doing things that show your love towards others can be awesome. When was the last time you felt like you loved yourself? If it was more than 7 days ago. Tell yourself that you love you and spend at least 5 minutes absorbing that feeling.

_____
_____
_____
_____
_____
_____
_____
_____
_____

Prayer: God, I am so glad you love me. Please continue to show me your goodness and mercy through the Love of Jesus. Amen.

What did you learn about yourself today?

Left border (vertical): You Are Worthy & GOD Lives In You

Right border (vertical): You Are Loved & You Are Chosen

Write or draw your expression/emotions above.

Day Twenty: Step Out of Your Comfort Zone

Make today special by doing something special, out of the ordinary or exciting for someone who is not in your everyday circle. This is a simple way to exchange love and spread kindness. In doing so, your heart will also be filled with joy!

Action: When was the last time someone did something for you that was unexpected or exciting? How did it make you feel?

Use your phone, Bible app, or physical Bible to read the following scriptures:

Proverbs 12:25; Luke 6:31; 1 Chronicles 19:2; Colossians 3:12

Do these scriptures call you to do something or change a current behavior? ☐ Yes ☐ No If yes, explain:

My Journey.

When you are comfortable there is a chance that you might miss out on new opportunities or blessings. When you are comfortable change can make you uncomfortable but it will result in growth.

_____
_____
_____
_____
_____
_____
_____
_____
_____
_____
_____
_____

Prayer: Please God keep me safe and in my right mind. Please let me continue to see your goodness and be able to share it with others without expecting something in return. Amen.

What did you learn about yourself today?

You Are Worthy & GOD Lives In You

You Are Loved & You Are Chosen

Write or draw your expression/emotions above.

Day Twenty One: Compassion & Mercy

When you have compassion in your heart you will also find the ability to love, the willingness to accept others for who they are, and the freedom to forgive those who may have wronged or hurt you. Let today be fueled by Compassion and Mercy!

Action: Who in your opinion has mistreated you, done you wrong, belittled you, or made you feel unworthy?

Write their name below:

_____

Use your phone, Bible app, or physical Bible to read the following scriptures:

Ephesians 2:4-5; Psalm 51:1-2; Matthew 6:14; Isiah 30:18

Do these scriptures call you to do something or change a current behavior? ☐ Yes ☐ No If yes, explain:

My Journey.

Write at least two sentences that will empower you to rise above the way the person whose name you wrote on the line made you feel.

When you are empowered and self-motivated, there is no one that can use words to harm you.

_____
_____
_____
_____
_____
_____
_____
_____
_____
_____
_____
_____

Prayer: Dear Lord, help me to forgive the people or person who distracted me from love, who hurt me verbally, mentally, or physically. Amen.

What did you learn about yourself today?

Left border (vertical): You Are Worthy & GOD Lives In You

Right border (vertical): You Are Loved & You Are Chosen

Write or draw your expression/emotions above.

Day Twenty Two: Praying for a Blessing

Today take a moment to pray that your day will be filled with blessings of Love, Peace, Understanding, Compassion, and Relaxation.

Wisdom Key: When you make prayer your first priority of the day, your day will be more balanced, productive, and meaningful. Meet God first thing in the morning and let him schedule your daily activity.

Use your phone, Bible app, or physical Bible to read the following scriptures:

Numbers 6:24-26; Psalm 20:4; Psalm 67:1; Ephesians 3:16; Isaiah 59:1

Do these scriptures call you to do something or change a current behavior? ☐ Yes ☐ No If yes, explain:

My Journey.

Do you think that it is selfish to pray for yourself?

☐ Yes ☐ No

It is not! The Lord wants the best for you and He delights in hearing your personal request and petitions.

Write down three things that you would like the Lord to do for you now or in the future.

_____
_____
_____
_____
_____
_____
_____
_____

Prayer: Thank you Lord for hearing me. Thank you for being available to me. If it is your will, please grant my prayer request as noted above. In Jesus' name. Amen.

What did you learn about yourself today?

Left border: You Are Worthy & GOD Lives In You

Right border: You Are Loved & You Are Chosen

Bottom: Write or draw your expression/emotions above.

Day Twenty Three: Share Your Smile

My Journey.

Tomorrow is not promised...so make the most of today. Share your smile and your laughter with someone, it has the ability to produce positive energy and to bring great joy.

Action: Laughter is also a good distraction. It can cause your perspective or mood to shift instantly.

Laughter is like exercise, it is necessary! List 3 things that make you smile and write the names of 3 people who make you laugh regularly.

Use your phone, Bible app, or physical Bible to read the following scriptures:

Job 8:21; Ecclesiastes 3:4; Psalm 30:11; Luke 6:21

Do these scriptures call you to do something or change a current behavior? ☐ Yes ☐ No If yes, explain:

Thinking back, has there been a time in your life when you laughed so hard that your belly or side began to hurt or you felt like you were going to wet your pants?

If so, was the thing that made you laugh really that funny or was it the way the person expressed themselves that caused you to laugh so hard?

_____
_____
_____
_____
_____
_____
_____
_____
_____
_____
_____

Prayer: Thank you Lord for the small things, they really make a difference. Amen.

What did you learn about yourself today?

You Are Worthy & GOD Lives In You

You Are Loved & You Are Chosen

Write or draw your expression/emotions above.

Day Twenty Four: Inhale to Exhale

My Journey.

Inhale confidence, exhale doubt or worry, and let love guide your action, attitude, and behavior.

Wisdom Key: Even when you feel less confident you can still be sure of who you are and why you were born. Do not let anxiety, doubt, worry or stress cause you to believe that you are not worthy of Love or a good life!

Use your phone, Bible app, or physical Bible to read the following scriptures:

Matthew 6:34; John 14:1; Colossians 3:14; Ephesians 5:2

Do these scriptures call you to do something or change a current behavior? ☐ Yes ☐ No If yes, explain:

Take at least 10 minutes to exhale, get rid of negative phrases or words that someone spoke to you. Inhale good thoughts about yourself, your life, your achievements, your growth, and your personal situation. The more positive you are the more opportunities will come to you.

_____
_____
_____
_____
_____
_____
_____
_____

Prayer: God, sometimes I forget to be thankful for just being me. Thank you for reminding me and helping me to change my view of myself. Amen.

What did you learn about yourself today?

You Are Worthy & GOD Lives In You

You Are Loved & You Are Chosen

Write or draw your expression/emotions above.

Day Twenty Five: Think Positive

If changing our eating habits have the ability to improve our health, reduce chances of disease, and over time create balance then the same is true of thinking. Changing your thought process has the ability to improve your attitude, behavior, and over time create balance. If you adopt positive thinking the outcome will be great for you and those around you.

Action: Do you control your thoughts or do your thoughts control you? Do you let others dictate how you feel? Who has more power them or God?

Use your phone, Bible app, or physical Bible to read the following scriptures:

Philippians 2:14-15; Proverbs 15:13; 2 Corinthians 5:17; Romans 15:5

Do these scriptures call you to do something or change a current behavior? ☐ Yes ☐ No
If yes, explain:

My Journey.

List three areas that you want to improve in within the next 30 days, such as overall attitude towards life, read more, spend more time with family, spend less time on social media, improve grades, lose weight etc. Then write two things that you can do immediately to meet the goal.

_____
_____
_____
_____
_____
_____
_____
_____
_____

Prayer: Lord help me to remove negative thoughts because I know that with you I can do all things, including changing my thinking! Amen.

What did you learn about yourself today?

You Are Worthy & GOD Lives In You

You Are Loved & You Are Chosen

Write or draw your expression/emotions above.

Day Twenty Six:
Surround Yourself with Positive People

Surround yourself with people who will motivate and encourage you to be the best you can be. Surround yourself with people who willingly love you and are brave and honest enough to tell you the truth even when it hurts. Love yourself enough to Embrace and Accept the TRUTH.

Action: How do you respond when someone points out your error or a flaw? Do you reject them or become angry? Do you give yourself time to reflect on what they said then evaluate or do you dismiss them and their comments immediately?

Use your phone, Bible app, or physical Bible to read the following scriptures:

Ecclesiastes 4:9; Job 6:14; Proverbs 18:24; Romans 12:10

Do these scriptures call you to do something or change a current behavior? ☐ Yes ☐ No If yes, explain:

My Journey.

Who are the people in your circle? Do you really know them? How much do you trust them? Are you willing to accept their criticism? Based on your answers you may need to take a deeper look at your circle and the people you allow into your private life. Everyone you let in your space is not meant to be trusted with the most intimate parts of your mind, body, or soul.

_____
_____
_____
_____
_____
_____
_____
_____

Prayer: Lord show me how to have friends and how to be a good friend to others. Amen.

What did you learn about yourself today?

You Are Worthy & GOD Lives In You

You Are Loved & You Are Chosen

Write or draw your expression/emotions above.

Day Twenty Seven: Be Free to Love and Be Loved

Love is patient and love is kind. It does not envy, it does not boast, it is not proud. It does not dishonor others, it is not self-seeking, it is not easily angered, it keeps no record of wrongs. Love does not delight in evil but rejoices with the truth. It always protects, it always trusts, it always hopes, and it always perseveres. Love never fails; therefore, feel free to truly express love, share love, and be loved!

Wisdom Key: Real love does not leave you empty even when the people involved do not regularly agree.

Use your phone, Bible app, or physical Bible to read the following scriptures:

1 Peter 4:8; 1 Corinthians 13:13; John 15:12

Do these scriptures call you to do something or change a current behavior? ☐ Yes ☐ No If yes, explain:

My Journey.

Loving someone may require you to extend forgiveness to them from time to time. In love relationships (family, friend, or romantic) do your best to be honest and open minded in order to create a healthy relationship.

How do you feel about that statement?

_____
_____
_____
_____
_____
_____
_____
_____
_____
_____

Prayer: God, I thank you for allowing me to experience love. As I mature, please help me to have, develop, and be in healthy relationships.

What did you learn about yourself today?

You Are Worthy & GODLy Lives In You

You Are Loved & You Are Chosen

Write or draw your expression/emotions above.

Day Twenty Eight: Create Your Own Outcome

Do challenges and struggle really make you stronger or do they lead to demise, hatred, and more strife? The answer lies within your perception, attitude, your choices, and where you channel energy.

Create positive outcomes by demonstrating positivity, respect, love, and good decision making.

Action: Who do you turn to when you need solid advice? How much do you trust them with your life and emotions?

Use your phone, Bible app, or physical Bible to read the following scriptures:

James 1:5; Titus 2:7; Hebrews 13:7-8; James 3:13; Proverbs 29:11

Do these scriptures call you to do something or change a current behavior? ☐ Yes ☐ No If yes, explain:

My Journey.

With God all things can be put together for your good. Without him life can take many unpleasant turns. When faced with making a decision, do you consult with God? Do you pray and ask for guidance or do you do what you feel is right then hope for the best?

_____
_____
_____
_____
_____
_____
_____
_____
_____
_____
_____

Prayer: God, I need you to guide me and help me make better decisions for myself, my life, and my family. I want to do better! Amen.

What did you learn about yourself today?

You Are Worthy & GODLives In You

You Are Loved & You Are Chosen

Write or draw your expression/emotions above.

Day Twenty Nine: An Amazing Day

My Journey.

How can you make today amazing for you and others? Be thankful for your blessings and be a blessing. Refrain from the entertainment of gossip and negative speak. Express love and forgiveness to yourself and others.

Today can and will be a good day for you!

Action: Write a sentence describing a time when someone either gossiped or told a lie on or about you. How did it feel and what did you do about it?

_____

Use your phone, Bible app, or physical Bible to read the following scriptures:

Ephesians 4:29; Exodus 23:1; James 4:11; Leviticus 19:11; Proverbs 12:22; Colossians 3:9

Do these scriptures call you to do something or change a current behavior? ☐ Yes ☐ No If yes, explain:

The words that come out of our mouths have the power to make people (including you) happy or sad. They have the power to create or destroy a good relationship. Think of 1 relationship that has been destroyed or that you walked away from. What could you have said or done differently to save that relationship?_____
_____
_____
_____
_____
_____
_____
_____
_____
_____
_____
_____

Prayer: Thank you for giving me a chance to honestly look at me. God, please help me to change for the better. Amen.

What did you learn about yourself today?

You Are Worthy & GOD Lives In You

You Are Loved & You Are Chosen

Write or draw your expression/emotions above.

Day Thirty: It's Worth It

My Journey.

Life may not be exactly what you want it to be or you may not be where you expected to be; but it's still worth the energy and effort to strive to be and do better.

Your future is not set based on your past. Your past has been full of lessons do not let those lessons discourage you!

Wisdom Key: You have the power within you to live a good life and to enjoy it to the fullest even when you feel disappointed or sad.

Use your phone, Bible app, or physical Bible to read the following scriptures:

Isiah 43:4; Zephaniah 3:17; 1 Timothy 2:3-4; Ephesians: 15-20; 1 John 1-9

Do these scriptures call you to do something or change a current behavior? ☐ Yes ☐ No If yes, explain:

You are worthy and God wants you to live your best life. You can live your best life, have fun and have a relationship with God.

Write one sentence that you can refer to when you make a mistake or disappoint the ones you love.

_____
_____
_____
_____
_____
_____
_____
_____
_____
_____
_____
_____

Prayer: Thank you Lord for walking with me on this journey and for giving me courage to complete this journal. Amen.

What did you learn about yourself today?

Left border: You Are Worthy & GOD Lives In You

Right border: You Are Loved & You Are Chosen

Write or draw your expression/emotions above.

COMMITMENT

This is going to sound narcissistic, but everything related to your **Balance** revolves around you! Therefore, you have the power to make a difference. Why? The answer is simple, you can create positive situations even when faced with negative occurrences. Question of the day... "Will you commit to making a difference?"

Today, make the decision to improve your life by making the following Personal Commitment Statements:

- I have the ability to **Create** an image of myself that I can be proud of.

- I will **Find** time to study the word of the Lord, receive positive messages, and continue to seek knowledge etc.

- I can make time to attend classes, workshops, and events that will present the opportunity to obtain, gain, and **Maintain** knowledge.

- I am empowered to use what I have, what I know, and what I have learned to **Impact** (affect) others and encourage myself.

- I have the power to make a difference and practice living a **Balanced** life!

Once you verbally and mentally say these statements or make the commitments you will have to take an honest look at yourself. Look for areas where you can continuously make changes and improvements. Remember continuous growth is encouraged as it will keep your mind challenged, elevate your knowledge base, and make you strive for more, all while keeping you grounded in your faith.

MOTIVATION

You are not alone, many of the people in your circle, family, or social media account need to work on improving certain areas of their lives too. Be patient with yourself this process will take time. When you can honestly admit that areas of your life are in need of improvement, change or renovation you can freely address or begin to deal with each workable issue. If you find time to increase knowledge and to study the Word you will be open to learning more and improving relationships across the board. A good way to learn more on a consistent basis is to commit to sharing the Word and information with others. I am not suggesting that you use the Word or information to beat up on people; however, I am suggesting that you use it as a tool to increase and strengthen your mind. As you help others you will learn to depend on God and leave each situation with a testimony!

You can be the balance that people in your circle, family, and social environment need to see or be influenced by.

If you completed this 30 Day journey, Congratulation! Do not let the Journey end. Keep reaching for more, strive to spend more time meditating on the Word, and always seek to be closer to God.

If you have not completed this 30 Day Journey yet you are here, go back to the page that you last read, pray for diligence, and complete the Journey. Remember, *"This journey is personal and no one but you will know if you have inserted the appropriate amount of effort, applied enough energy, or if you grew from past experiences."* Completing what you start is a good way to build character and, in this case, if you do not complete the journey you may miss out on something really important, discovering you! The number of times you start something is not as important as the number of times you complete something.

FINAL PRAYER

Dear Lord,

If there is anything that was restricting me or distracting me from you, I ask that you remove it. Allow me to freely give myself to you so that I can graciously experience a life full of your blessings and mercy. I ask that you present me with the tools needed to fully express forgiveness towards myself and others. I ask that you heal me and use my issues to draw me closer to you; so that I will continuously depend on you for strength, guidance, and hope.

In Jesus Name I humbly submit this request into your loving Kingdom!

The following space can be used to write your own personal final prayer.

_____

_____

_____

_____

_____

_____

_____

_____

_____

_____

CONCLUSION

You must have a foundation, prayer life, honest relationships, and compassion in your heart. You must have an open and forgiving heart so that when you or the people around you make a mistake it does not feel like the end.

Resources are all around you but you may have to FIND time to utilize them. You may need to CREATE an opportunity to tap into those resources.

You have the power to live a life free of negativity. You have the power to be a better person. You have the power to be impactful in your life and the lives of others. You have the power to make a difference!

Information

To find out more about our publications and community work please check our websites:

WWW.JAAZWORLD.COM has a full body of information and detail of services offered such as Creative Nspiration, Handcrafted Greeting Cards, Spiritual resources, Community Services, and various creative expressions by the Author.

Visit WWW.JAAZWORLD.WIXSITE.COM/INSPIRE or scan the box below for more Jaaz Nspiration. You will find that our site promotes good vibes and offers consistent Nspirational motivation based on Christian Foundation.

WWW.JNOUTREACH.ORG is where you can find more information on our Community services and Literacy Programs.

Previous Publications

Jaaz Nspirations:

Impacting Lives and Making a Difference (2018)

My Prayers Have the Power to Make a Difference (2019)

For autographed copies send an email to Jacque@jaazworld.com

Upcoming Publications

Jaaz Nspiration Volume 2

The Path We Pave (Men's Prayer Book)

Advertisements

Contact JN Notary at JN@sfnorris.org for notary service in California
For custom handcrafted greeting cards and 8x8 Canvas gifts go to: JAAZWORLD.COM/SHOP OR send an email to jacque@jaazworld.com
To hear Nspirational messages in under 5 minutes go to: JAAZWORLD.COM/PODCAST or ANCHOR.FM/JACQUELINE-NORRIS
To schedule Nspiration sessions or Life Coaching Sessions go to: WWW.JAAZWORLD.COM/BOOK-ONLINE
To purchase previous Jaaz Nspiration publications go to: WWW.JAAZWORLD.COM/PUBLICATIONS
For Virtual Professional Services contact jaazworld@gmail.com

www.ingramcontent.com/pod-product-compliance
Lightning Source LLC
LaVergne TN
LVHW051158080426
835508LV00021B/2681